ANGLO-SA
CAMBRIDGE⌄ı ııκL

Introduction

Anglo-Saxon Cambridgeshire covers the period betweeen D.M. Browne's *Roman Cambridgeshire* and H.C. Darby's *Medieval Cambridgeshire*; that is, it falls between the well-documented Roman and Norman conquests and covers the time when Germanic mercenaries and invaders and the remnants of Roman Britain became the English nation. This period saw the English settlement of the so-called Dark Ages, the long and eventually unsuccessful struggles against the Danes and the creation of a national political and administrative system with Christian values and culture. The major achievement, however, was the establishment of nearly all the towns, villages and farmland of modern England.

Because this book is concerned with Cambridgeshire it can deal only fleetingly with national developments and the influences of the Continent and its archaeological bias leads to greater concentration on physical remains rather than the written record which has contributed so much to lifting Anglo-Saxon studies from the conjectural reconstructions of earlier times. Selection, however, is necessary in a work of this length, for possible sources include historical documents, art history, philology, numismatics, place-name studies, literature, architecture, historical geography, excavations, artifacts and standing monuments and it is not possible to describe adequately all of these. I have therefore chosen to concentrate on aspects that are well represented in Cambridgeshire and illuminate our understanding of life and achievements in this period. Where possible I have used examples which can be visited to-day or have left a detectable impact on our surroundings.

Political Background

Cambridgeshire has no particular political history of its own in the early years of this period for it did not form part of any one of the great Saxon kingdoms. Instead, the area of the modern county until the ninth century fell between the land of the East Angles, Mercians (to the north), Middle Angles (to the

3

west), East Saxons (in Hertfordshire and Essex), and the Gyrwa, a little-known tribe who seem to have inhabited the Fenlands between Stamford and Wisbech. Of these the most powerful were the East Angles and the Mercians, who merged with the Middle Angles in the seventh century, and the boundaries of their territories fluctuated to and fro across Cambridgeshire. Campaigns across the county must have been quite common and the dykes are a physical reminder of such wars. It is unlikely that the people would feel much allegiance to any one kingdom: this is reflected in their lack of resistance to the Danes and the ease with which the county became a rather fringe part of the Danelaw in the ninth century and then reverted to English rule fifty years later, retaining scarcely any trace of Danish influence. From the tenth century however, eastern England was divided into shires and it becomes possible to write of 'Cambridgeshire', 'Huntingdonshire' and the 'Soke of Peterborough' as political entities although their boundaries were only fixed for the convenience of tenth century local government.

In describing the political development of Cambridgeshire, one is involved in the history of the rest of England and the intricate series of campaigns, battles, conquests, and kings with which our written sources are mostly preoccupied, as well as two major influxes of population. The fifth and sixth centuries AD are still poorly understood, for our historical sources dealing with this period were either written down at a later date, such as the accounts of Bede and the *Anglo-Saxon Chronicle*, or were little concerned with historical aspects of the English settlement. In these years Germanic tribes including the traditional Angles, Saxons and Jutes of Bede's *History* entered Britain, first as raiders, then as mercenaries who received land in return for protecting the Romano-British against other invaders, and finally as families of farmers who took over as much land as they could. The settlers of Cambridgeshire arrived by sea via the Wash and the Fenland rivers, spreading out along the fen margins and river valleys.

Resistance to the invaders was strong in the west of England where, for example, Arthur led a British revival in the late fifth century which kept the Saxons at bay until the mid sixth century, but in the regions around Cambridgeshire the Saxons arrived very early, probably starting in the late fourth century, and to judge by the evidence of the cemeteries there were large and stable communities along the Cam and to a lesser extent the Ouse and Nene valleys from the early fifth century onwards. Their relationships with the native Romano-British people cannot have been very friendly but the archaeological evidence points to a considerable period of co-existence; in Cambridge, for example, the large cemetery found on St John's cricket field was obviously in use by pagan Saxons during the occupation of the walled town by urbanised Romano-Britons, while at Orton Longueville, near Peterborough, fifth century Saxon occupation was found all round the

R. D. BEACHAM

ANGLO-SAXON CAMBRIDGESHIRE

ALISON TAYLOR

THE OLEANDER PRESS OF CAMBRIDGE

The Oleander Press
17 Stansgate Avenue
Cambridge CB2 2QZ

ISBN 0 900891 07 6

Cover illustration:
Large square-headed brooch from Haslingfield (length 17cms).
(*photo D. Hall*)

Title page illustration:
A possible reconstruction of a Saxon house at St. Neots.

Designed by Ron Jones

Printed and bound by The Burlington Press, Foxton.

contemporary Roman farm site. Roman settlement in suitable areas was so intensive, however, that many of their farms must have been taken over by force while their owners fled or were slain. The pressure on land must have been considerable, for there seems to have been subsidence in the fens added to climatic deterioration, and without the Roman system of organized drainage the Fenlands went out of cultivation. The nature of the fens at this time is graphically described by Felix, an eighth century monk. "There is in Britain a fen of immense size, which begins from the river Granta not far from the city which is called Granteceaster. There are immense marshes, now a black pool of water, now foul running streams, and also many islands, and reeds, and hillocks, and thickets, and with manifold windings wide and long it continues up to the north sea." Although the Saxons were willing to farm some marginal land, such as the sandy heaths just east of Cambridgeshire, their settlement of the wooded claylands had not begun in this early period. By the early sixth century all aspects of Romano-British culture were absent from Cambridgeshire, whatever had become of the people and their descendants.

During the seventh century much of Cambridgeshire was captured by Redwald, the mighty East Anglian king who is possibly buried at Sutton Hoo, and it was then ravaged again by the Mercians who had absorbed the kingdom of the Middle Angles. Most of the campaigns of this time are undocumented and little understood but it seems that the Cam was a frontier for much of the period. The Fens were very thinly settled and the Isle of Ely was early recognised as a separate district that acted as a border march for East Anglia. In the mid seventh century it was ruled by Tonbert who married the East Anglian princess Etheldreda. It was she who founded the monastery at Ely in 673 and the Isle became a permanent endowment for the religious house retaining governmental independence.

The years between the late seventh and the middle ninth centuries were relatively peaceful and the conversion to Christianity was officially complete. This is therefore a great period for the foundation of the early religious houses. During the ninth century, however, the Danes began invading along the coasts and in 866 the *Anglo-Saxon Chronicle* describes how there "came a large heathen army into England and fixed their winter quarters in East Anglia where they were soon horsed and the inhabitants made peace with them". After successive attacks on Northumbria and Mercia they returned to winter quarters at Thetford in 870. King Edmund the Martyr led the Saxons against them but was defeated and slain and after this victory they were able to ravage unchecked. The *Anglo-Saxon Chronicle* records that they "came to Medhamstede (Peterborough) burning and breaking and slaying abbots and monks and all that they found. They made such havoc there that a monastery which was before full rich, was now reduced to nothing". In 871 they moved on to Wessex where Alfred and his brother Ethelred were able to defeat them, but they continued to raid elsewhere and in 875 "a vast army" spent a year in Cambridge.

The efforts of Alfred and Wessex eventually ended the raids of the Danes although they could not remove their presence. The result was Alfred and Guthrum's Pact in 886 which defined an area of eastern England, including Cambridgeshire, as the 'Danelaw' where Danish settlers were to farm unmolested, although the rights of the Saxons in that area were protected. The area of modern Cambridgeshire therefore was under Danish control until the reconquest by Alfred's son Edward in 921. According to the *Anglo-Saxon Chronicle* sporadic fighting continued, with Huntingdon in particular being fortified alternately by the Danes and the English, but eventually the area came under the control of the Wessex, or as they can now be called, English kings.

During the reigns of Edward (899-925) and Athelstan (925-939), the Wessex system of shires was adopted in East Anglia, with boundaries fixed around territories based on existing important towns which would normally be fortified. Later the shires were subdivided into hundreds for the purposes of justice, taxation and police, but the shires were to have the longest history in local government. Their significance in this period is not clear but evidently in battle they fought as a unit, for the *Anglo-Saxon Chronicle* records that the men of Cambridgeshire stood firm while East Angles fled in yet another battle with the Danes.

After Edward's reign life in Cambridgeshire was fairly peaceful, particularly during the reign of Edgar the Peaceable (957-975), when the great Saxon religious houses were founded or re-founded and literature and the arts flourished. Then, in the late tenth century, Danish raids began again and this time coincided with the reign of one of the very few unsatisfactory Saxon kings, Ethelred, known as "the Unready", and the attacks became so serious that a large army defeated the Saxons in East Anglia and then "plundered and burned three months; and then proceeded further into the wild fens, slaying both men and cattle and burning throughout the fens. Thetford also they burned and Cambridge". By 1011 Ethelred tried to buy off the Danes after they had overrun eighteen counties, including Cambridge-shire and half Huntingdonshire, but he continued to be defeated. In 1016 the Danish leader Cnut was accepted as king after Ethelred had fled to France and his son Edmund Ironside had been killed, leaving only infant heirs. Cnut swore to uphold English laws and to rule with the advice of Christian bishops, and under him and his Danish and Saxon successors England was peacefully governed until 1066 when William, himself of Viking descent, made the final conquest.

Rural Settlements

The pattern of settlement by the earliest Saxons can be traced at present only by the distribution of pagan cemeteries, which follow a predictable route along the river valleys, especially that of the Cam, with a few outlying sites along the edge of the Fens. These settlers, therefore, were joining the Romano-British population on the area that had been preferred for settlements since agriculture had been started in Cambridgeshire, and it is not surprising that so many Roman sites contain at least a few sherds of the plain handmade early Saxon pottery. By the end of the Saxon period, however, when Domesday Book was written, the great majority of our modern villages were in existence; in other words, late Saxon settlement had spread fairly evenly across the whole landscape except for uninhabitable land such as the peat fens and stretches of the chalk where there was no water. This should not be construed as a shift in population, for the gravel terraces and fen edges continued to be favoured areas, but we do have to recognise that at some stage after pagan cemeteries had gone out of use during the seventh century and before parish boundaries became fixed (which probably occurred in most cases during the administrative reforms of the tenth century), several hundred new villages and their attendant fields were created from the forests. These years coincided with Danish attacks, suggesting that these new immigrants more than made up in numbers for those that perished in the fighting and that the devastation they caused acted as a stimulus to expansion.

The form of these new villages is now open to much debate although in the past the nucleated village which had one settlement in each parish clustered round a green and complete with manor house and church was the accepted picture for this part of Britain. Domesday Book was concerned with ownership and resources of villages but not with their layout and probably gives a misleading picture by describing groups· of settlements under their parish name without reference to outlying hamlets, and the later pattern of growth for the main villages at the expense of the minor settlements in later medieval and modern times reinforces opinions on this pattern. Recent work, however, especially by C.C. Taylor in south Cambridgeshire has shown that many apparently normal nucleated villages originally contained several scattered settlements and the period when the classic medieval layout was organised is still unknown. Normal excavation methods are unlikely to be very helpful because work on such a large scale is necessary and because so much evidence is lost beneath modern villages, although observations of the date ranges of occupation material from a variety of locations where settlements can be differentiated by manuring would be valuable.

Excavations which have produced vital evidence regarding Saxon rural settlements are those on sites which went out of use in later times and where the ephemeral traces of timber buildings and their attendant structures and artifacts have been uncovered. Houses from the early Saxon period are rare and the only ones discovered so far are those described as 'grubenhäuser' or pit dwellings. These consist of hollows in the ground with posts at each end. They have been variously interpreted as workshops, used in particular for weaving, as houses for slaves, sleeping sheds and as normal living quarters which could have been made comfortable with plank floors at ground levels and vertical timber walls, examples of which have been reconstructed at West Stow in Suffolk. Such structures of course survive much better in the archaeological record than normal timber buildings which can only be recognized by post holes and slots for sleeper beams, and it is difficult to believe that people would live in unnecessarily small or squalid huts on permanent sites when we know that their carpenters were capable of building large halls, ships and, in the later periods, churches. Literary evidence makes it clear that social life as well as administration and culture were centred on the great halls and it seems likely that most settlements would contain one such structure, but at the moment we can only look at the evidence which is available.

Three early Saxon huts were excavated at Waterbeach,[1] each dug about 2ft into the ground. They were sub-rectangular and one, which was approximately 10ft by 8ft, had a single post hole in the centre of each short side to support a ridge pole. Finds from the huts included some Roman objects but were mostly pagan Saxon. T.C. Lethbridge, the excavator, discovered glass beads, bone pins, ivory rings, a bronze needle, perforated boar's tusk, bone awl, iron nails, pottery spindle whorls, bronze fragments, sheep, ox, pig and dog bones as well as plain, handmade pottery.

At Houghton[2] one small stray hut of a similar date was excavated. It proved to be 5ft 8ins by 6ft 5ins with a central post hole and another on the south side. There was an entrance on the east and a protruding rectangle on the west which was thought to be a latrine. Loom weights, a knife, broken pot, wattle and daub, horn cores and broken rib bones were scattered throughout the hut which seems to have been some sort of workshop. A similar dwelling also occurred on an excavation at Grantchester and was dated by a brooch and some pottery to around 500 AD.

Excavations at Maxey[3] on a middle Saxon site were on a more satisfactory scale. No 'pit dwellings' were found but there were seven rectangular timber buildings, ranging from 30ft to 50ft long and 16ft to 20ft wide. All were supported on upright posts, some of which were set in trenches, others in individual post holes joined by wall trenches and one had a central beam slot to contain roof supports. It seems that most of the walls had individual posts with wattle and daub panels between them, but one structure had close set uprights, perhaps with planks between them. There was little evidence concerning the function of these buildings but they were apparently not long-houses with animals and habitation under the same roof. Other slight timber structures, hearths and many pits were found around the houses. Many of the pits seem to have been dug and then left open. They were possibly just used as quarries, for they contained no more rubbish than would accumulate in any hollow and they were unsuitable for storage or for wells. Some had post holes around them or wicker structures inside and these were probably used as small covered cellars. There were also three fire-pits.

Not enough of the site was recovered to make generalisations about the plan of the village or the functions of the structures, but the main buildings clearly were arranged around a central area which contained only a few pits and hearths, within which there was a completely open area which can be interpreted as either a farm yard or a village green. P.V. Addyman, the excavator, considered that the site had probably been a peasant village with some individual buildings with special functions which could be either communal or manorial depending on how feudal society had become. The buildings were not renewed or repaired and cannot have been very long lived, and the settlement must have shifted either westwards towards the church or eastwards towards the modern village. The economy at Maxey was based on grain, cattle and sheep or goats to judge by the quern stones and bones found and there were also a few horse and pig bones and the eggs and bones of wild fowl. Pottery found on the site was local handmade ware. The only imported goods were whetstones and lava querns from Germany, for iron was smelted on the site to judge from the large quantities of slag found. Other artifacts included iron knives, nails, a pair of shears and an arrowhead, bronze tag-ends and two bronze pins, a bone comb, bone pin and an object described as a 'thread picker'.

An important late Saxon site was noticed during gravel workings near Little Paxton[4] and emergency excavations were carried out that showed that there was a late ninth century to early eleventh century settlement extending for a third of a mile. There were many settings of post holes and slots suggesting structures but no really acceptable buildings could be discerned. There were also many rubbish pits and wells and two enclosures which did not seem to bound any particular features. A wide drove-way had trenches leading away from it, suggesting the demarcations of fields or the limits of holdings within the settlement. It is possible this village shifted to Little Paxton some time near the Conquest, but it is more likely that it was a separate hamlet or else a large estate within the parish. Pottery from the site was nearly all local St Neots ware with scarcely any imported sherds, and it all dated to the pre-Conquest period. Lava querns and a whetstone had been imported, as usual, and the other simple objects found were also very similar to those common throughout the Saxon period, including pins, knives, a bronze strap end, buckle plates, (one attached to an iron buckle), a bone pin and 'thread picker' and a comb.

Investigations following the ploughing of a moated site at Southoe[5] uncovered a very different late Saxon site. There appeared to be a pit dwelling 6ft by 3ft 9ins and 6ft deep with post holes on both sides of one end, the other end being much disturbed. The late Saxon pottery on the site included yellow glazed Stamford ware suggesting there was a higher class of dwelling nearby that had not survived. The animal bones were also rather unusual for they included remains from many ducks, oysters, mussels, geese and two chickens.

Another type of building somewhat similar to one found in St Neots was uncovered near Buckden[6] in 1961 when the bypass on the A1 was being constructed. The house was 'boat-shaped' with two beam slots 46ft long which bulged outwards giving a shape 17ft wide in the centre and 15ft wide at the ends. The straight end walls were supported by fairly regular rows of post holes. All the pottery found was of the eleventh century. The circumstances of the excavation made it impossible to look for other features near the house.

Place Names

When Domesday Book was written nearly all our villages were in existence and were called by names recognisably similar to those they still hold. Many field and road names were also current and so were names of most topographical features such as hills and rivers. Apart from topographical features the vast majority of these names are Anglo-Saxon, and so theoretically we should be able to decipher a whole series of descriptive phrases from the names given to each of the villages when first they were recognised as separate settlements. Unfortunately there are so many problems and contradictions that place-name evidence remains one of our most difficult and sometimes misleading sources.

The first difficulty is that of simple interpretation, for the first record of most names is that written down by a Norman scribe several hundred years after it was first used and after the Saxon language itself had changed greatly. Then there are the problems of why particular names were given, and by whom. People do not need names for their own villages but will attach descriptions to surrounding settlements, and they do not necessarily use features typical of the landscape but are more likely to pick something unusual to distinguish one village from the next. We cannot therefore be sure that a name is a true reflection of the language, date and environment of a particular settlement. Political upheavals must also have led to the loss of many villages and the foundations of new ones. These are some of the reasons why we can search place names in vain for convincing evidence of two settlement factors of which we can be fairly certain, firstly that there was considerable very early settlement in this area, probably involving the absorption and co-existence of many British peoples, and secondly that Cambridgeshire was administered and settled by the Danes for nearly fifty years.

British village names are extremely rare although the river names Ouse, Granta ('muddy' or 'fen river'), Rhee (simply 'at the river'), Kennet, and Nene all seem to be British survivals. Chatteris and Chettisham, both in the Fens away from main settlement areas, are probably British names including the word 'cet' meaning a wood. Walworth, near Horningsea, means 'enclosure of the Britons' and it has been suggested that Comberton was 'a village of the Cumbrians', i.e. Welsh or Britons.

Many early Saxon settlements are suggested by personal names together with the element 'inga' meaning 'people of . . . . '. These are not common in Cambridgeshire and do not seem to lie in areas one would expect to find such settlement on topographical or archaeological grounds. Good examples are Kirtling, Yelling, Gidding, Wittering, Wintringham, Willingham and Dullingham. Other early names are those which contain elements known to have gone out of use in the early years, such as March, Mepal, Malton and Lymage, but again such names are exceptional and are not attached to significant villages. One important early name, however is Earith, meaning 'muddy landing place', for this is indeed one of the first possible landing places for travellers via the Wash and Ouse.

For the later Saxon names 'ham' and 'ton' are common, both apparently meaning any sort of village community. 'Ham' names are normally earlier than 'tons', but there are plenty of exceptions. Hinxton and Sawston, for example, are early, while Newnham and West Wickham are obviously late.

One informative aspect of later place names is the 'west' element in a group of villages in south east Cambridgeshire. These villages, Westley Waterless, Weston Colville, West Wratting and West Wickham, all lie on an area of previously forested clayland that had been little occupied by previous peoples and therefore they can be seen as classic 'secondary settlements' created by people moving out from expanding villages to reclaim the virgin forests. Logically they must have been settled and named by parent villages to the east which means the forest of Suffolk rather than the Icknield Way.

We also have a few tribal names such as Saxon Street, Swaffham (after the Swabians) and Anglesey. Swavesey, however, another possibility, seems to be the personal name 'Swaefa' together with 'hythe' or landing place.

The Scandinavian influence on Cambridgeshire place-names is slight, and where Danish personal names do occur they are often mixed with a Saxon ending such as 'ton' as in Caxton and Croxton which were named after men named Kakkr and Krokr. The only pure Danish names are Bourn (stream), Toft (site of a house and its buildings), Toseland and Sibthorpe. This last example is one of the very few 'thorpe' names and these occur only in the north of the county and there are no 'by' names, although these are both very common elements in areas of the Danelaw such as Yorkshire and Lincolnshire where Danes settled in large numbers. 'Gate', the Danish word for road, is used in northern parts of Cambridgeshire, for example at Fengate, and seems to be interchangeable with Saxon terms, for at Tydd St Giles both Kirkgate and Church Street occur, although their meaning is identical.

Environmental evidence is preserved in some names. Obvious examples are the frequent Fenland villages ending in 'ey' or 'is'. These can be confusing for they can be derived from 'ge' (district) as in Ely, 'ea' (river) or 'eg' (island), these last two being extremely common in fenland topography. In the east and west of Cambridgeshire on the clay soils woodland place-names are naturally very common. Apart from the obvious examples, such as 'ley' meaning either a wood or clearing, there are 'hay' meaning an enclosure or enclosed wood, 'stubbing' and 'stocking' signifying land cleared of tree stumps, and 'wilds', meaning the same as weald, a stretch of woodland, all pointing to the existence of a wooded landscape well into the Saxon period.

Descriptive place-names recall features or activities of local interest. Shippea and Quy were islands where sheep and cows were kept, Manea has 'well watered land held in common', Fowlmere was the 'home of wild fowl' and Guilden Morden was 'golden' i.e. 'rich, productive'. 'Bury' can mean homestead or it might refer to ancient fortifications, as at Wandlebury and Arbury, while 'low' often suggests a notable burial mound, as at Limlow Hill and Thriplow. Mentions of features such as trees, as at Bythorn, are not usually informative, but Sapley near Huntingdon seems to mean 'fir-tree clearing' which is a surprising reference to this sort of wood at this date.

Urban Settlements

Settlements which grew into towns in Saxon times were nearly all administrative centres or particularly well situated to engage in trade, usually involving international exchanges. Wisbech had a coastal position but, even though it warranted fortifying with a Norman castle there is no evidence that it achieved significance as a town in Saxon times. Peterborough and Ely were still almost entirely religious centres and St Ives was the village of Slepe. Only Huntingdon and Cambridge therefore are really acceptable as Saxon trading and administrative centres and, as so little is so far known about Huntingdon, I have concentrated on Cambridge. I have also described St Neots in this chapter more because of its later history and because so much is known about it, than because of its urban characteristics at this time.

Cambridge

In Cambridge[7,8] at the end of the Roman period there were four major

12

roads converging on a small walled town on the hill on the north side of the river commanding a river crossing where a bridge had probably been built. Evidence for the town's development during the next five hundred years relies on stray historical references and very disturbed archaeological sites but during Edgar's reign (957-975) we can recognise the outlines of a flourishing county town. The two most important aspects of a town's history are probably how and when it developed various urban characteristics, and where the settlement was centred and spread during its development. Cambridge is particularly interesting in this second aspect because of the shift from the Roman town on the north side of the river to the late Saxon and modern town centred on Market Hill south of the river. To follow this change, which seems to be a gradual shift of emphasis perhaps with deliberate urban planning at one stage, we have to plot the distribution of archaeological sites and finds. This is a difficult and unsatisfactory process because a town that has been continually and densely occupied up to the present day will have normally disturbed most of its earliest levels, leaving the archaeologist with stray finds, residual material mixed with later features and the bottom layers of occasional pits and wells. Exceptions are the very easily recognisable sites that attracted the attention of early antiquaries, the most notable of which are pagan cemeteries, and sites which for some reason avoided development in later periods, such as part of the Roman town on Castle Hill opposite Shire Hall. Neither of these types of site is likely to be typical of the main settlement.

Nearly all our evidence concerning the very early settlement derives from the pagan cemeteries. These are:

1. St John's College cricket field. A mixed inhumation and cremation cemetery, with over two hundred cinerary urns and thirty skeletons excavated and hundreds of others known to have been destroyed, dating from the mid fifth to the early seventh century, excavated in 1888. The grave goods were mostly pots of many forms, brooches and other decorative bronze objects. One brooch was inlaid with silver and another with glass or garnets. Stray burials on Grange Road and Madingley Road are probably part of this cemetery.

2. River Cam. Many decorative cinerary urns have been dredged from the river near Magdalene Bridge, possibly because its later course cut through a cemetery.

3. Newnham Croft. Two inhumations date to the mid sixth century with wrist guards and four brooches. Urns and spears found here were probably connected with these burials.

Scattered finds or isolated burials have also turned up from Coldham Common, Mill Road, Newmarket Road, Jesus Lane, Sidney Street, Rose

Crescent (which included spears, knives, shield bosses, a buckle and fragments of decorated pottery) and Trinity Hall.

This cemetery evidence seems to show a scattered population occurring only incidentally in the medieval centre with a great majority of its burials on one site north of the river but outside the Roman town. There is virtually no evidence of early habitation and no reason to suppose that the cemeteries (which are no different in character from those found elsewhere on the Cam gravels and are scarcely more concentrated than in other highly favoured areas) represented an urban settlement or any continuity with the Roman town. The early settlers were not normally attracted by towns or by living in large numbers and we also have the evidence of Bede who tells the story of how, when the monks of Ely wanted a suitable coffin for St Etheldreda in 695 they found a stone sarcophagus "near the walls of a little deserted city called by the English Granta Caestir". He was writing in Yorkshire but he died only thirty years later and is unlikely to have been ignorant of a town of any significance, so there seems no reason to dismiss his evidence.

Probably Cambridge's military position on the Cam crossing was important during the Mercian and East Anglian campaigns and Felix, who died in 730, refers to a 'Castellum' near the Granta which is most likely to refer to a defended hill top point, not to a prosperous valley settlement. The first known period of peace and stability was under Offa (757-796). He brought East Anglia under his control, became famous for fostering international contacts and trade and would have been very likely to appreciate the advantages of a bridge over the river at this point. Certainly when next there is a historical mention the settlement is called 'Granta Brycge', proving the existence of a bridge, which was felt to be the most important element of the town. The occasion of this mention is the occupation by the Danish army in 875, described by the *Anglo-Saxon Chronicle*. This occupation also suggests that Cambridge was the most important settlement in the area and that its strategic importance was considerable. It remained part of the Danelaw apparently without further incident until 921. Edward proceeded to organise most of England into counties and, established fortified 'burhs'. Near the Danelaw boundary the 'burhs' were normally based on existing towns which thus gained military and administrative status and became the county town of the areas named after them such as Bedfordshire, Huntingdonshire, Cambridgeshire, Hertfordshire. It was quite probably Edward who built the King's Ditch which, apart from suburbs such as Barnwell and Newnham, was to remain the effective town boundary until the nineteenth century. He is known as an energetic town planner and may have been directly responsible for laying out an organised town south of the river in addition to his indirect influence in defending an administrative market centre on the area of land most obviously suited for civilian growth. As Edward was probably responsible

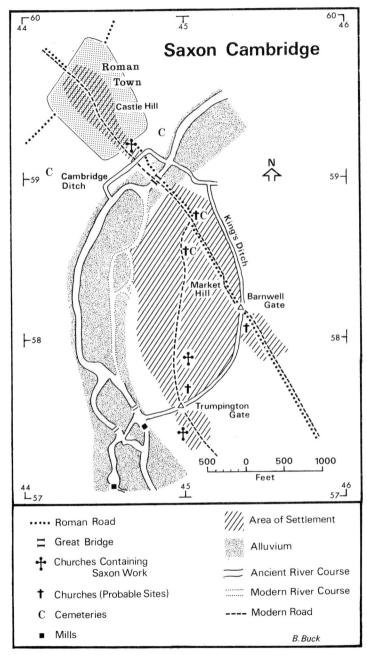

1. Saxon Cambridge (*drawn by B. Buck, based mainly on Addyman & Biddle, 1965*).

2. A Saxon grave-slab, probably made in Cambridge, built into Little Shelford church (*photo D. Hall*).

for a similar development in Huntingdon we can recognise him as the most important figure in the creation of Cambridgeshire towns. By Edgar's reign (957-975) Cambridge officially had a court, a market and a mint (from which many coins have been discovered), it was fortified and was the centre of the new county of Grantabricshire which was to continue as 'Cambridgeshire' until its expansion in 1974.

The town's potential as a trading centre with access to the Wash was probably the main element in its growth over the next few years and Irish traders are reported in the late tenth century. Cnut led further Viking invasions (which this time succeeded in conquering England) and he burnt Cambridge in spite of the recorded "heroic resistance" by the men of Cambridgeshire. But this had little impact on the town's growth, and Domesday Book and the architectural and archaeological remains enable us to describe many features of the town by the end of the Saxon period.

There was a population around 2,000, of whom about a third lived on the north side of the river and the boundaries of the town were the King's and Cambridge Ditches. Finds of late Saxon pottery suggest that occupation was spread down Castle Hill and throughout most of the habitable land with suburban settlements beyond the Barnwell and Trumpington Gates. These gates may have been in existence for their positions must already have been important. There were four mills, of which the probable positions of three are known, and there is evidence for ten churches although for five of these the evidence is conjectural. High quality decoratively carved grave-slabs suggest there was a school of skilled craftsmen working there, and a "guild of thegns" is also recorded. There was a mint employing at least three moneyers and the town had its own court. The Normans were to make Cambridge a military stronghold again and were to found the first religious houses, and then later the university was to arrive, but it was the Saxons who had created Cambridge as a manufacturing market town servicing the surrounding countryside and linking it with international trade. Both the southern and northern sectors of the town were occupied, but Helen Cam is no doubt right in her conclusion that by 1086 the southern settlement was considerably more wealthy and populous than the northern.

St. Neots

Unlike Cambridge, St Neots was not apparently important as an urban administrative centre in the Saxon period and it is scarcely mentioned in the historic record, but archaeological work by C.F. Tebbutt in 1929-1932 and P.V. Addyman in 1961 has shown that there was a sizeable, well laid-out settlement with many indications of domestic industries in the late Saxon period obviously suited to grow into a flourishing market town, and with a religious house that would later become the backbone of the town's development.

The geographical position of St Neots was ideally suited to a trading centre. The Ouse was navigable this far and it was the obvious crossing point linking Cambridge, Bedford, Kimbolton and Huntingdon. It is noticeable, however, that the Saxon town was not sited near the crossing point of the river but on land that was more suitable for agriculture and habitation, being well drained, fertile and supplied with water from the Hen and Fox Brooks. It was not until the Middle Ages, when trade and the priory were the most important elements of the town's economy, that the main settlement was moved to the modern centre.

The 1929-32 excavations of C.F. Tebbutt were extremely important to the archaeological world because the 'pit dwellings' he discovered were among the first to be recognised in England and at the time were thought to be the normal Saxon dwellings. This was also the site where St Neots ware was first identified and christened. Other finds included rubbish pits, ditches, (possibly for drainage), clay loom weights, lava querns from Germany, bone combs and assorted iron objects. The excavations were very much rescue work carried out by a young amateur while gravel quarrying was in progress at a time when Saxon habitation sites were almost unknown, but the basis for the early history of St Neots was now laid.

Our picture of Saxon St Neots became clearer in 1961 when house building was planned near the previous excavations.[9] P.V. Addyman excavated a further area to see if any Saxon occupation was still undisturbed. He found that much had been destroyed by medieval and post-medieval features but he was able to excavate one large Saxon timber building and parts of five or six more together with a number of ditches, trenches and pits. One of the buildings, which was approximately 38ft. by 20ft., was slightly "boat shaped" and the suggested reconstruction is shown below. No building materials were found apart from a few fragments of burnt daub, and so the houses were presumably roofed with thatch or shingles and the timbers fixed with carpentered or pegged joints, as no nails were found. Some of the house timbers had been placed in rows of post holes, but most were morticed into ground sills (as illustrated), and as this seems to be a common technique and will obviously leave very little trace in the archaeological record, it is easy to see why such buildings are so rarely recognised.

No 'pit houses' like those found by C.F. Tebbutt occurred on this excavation, so there was no opportunity to examine these structures with modern techniques, but the original descriptions strongly support the idea that some of them were indeed used for habitation even if the population were at the same time erecting the sophisticated airy halls of the later excavations, for many hearths were found in the 'pits', one contained regular post hole fittings for roof supports, and another many broken loom weights. The most likely explanation, therefore, is that the two excavators found separate parts of a properly laid-out settlement, with houses in one quarter and the workshops, including weaving sheds, in another.

The economy was concerned chiefly with agriculture. Many animal bones were found and the growing of grain is demonstrated by quern stones and one ploughshare. The lumps of slag and the clay loom weights show that iron-working and weaving were carried out, but these were normally domestic crafts at this time and need not imply any urbanisation or trade. The only intriguing hint of manufacturing activity on a larger scale were two pits which the excavator thought might have been 'pit kilns' used in producing St Neots ware which would be the only evidence we have for this important industry and trade. No exotic items or signs of wealth were found and there is no reason to think that the town was yet taking advantage of its geographical position as a likely market centre.

The extent of the settlement has been worked out from observations of Saxon pottery scatters, by the negative evidence of C.F. Tebbutt who watched construction work in St Neots for over forty years but found no late Saxon pottery in the medieval layers of the rest of the town, and by the discovery and excavation in 1964 of a substantial wet defensive ditch by G.T. Rudd and C.F. Tebbutt. This ditch ran along Cambridge Street and Church Street and quite probably joined up with Fox Brook to give a continuous defence and boundary around a settlement of about 28 acres, probably with occupations spreading a little to the east.

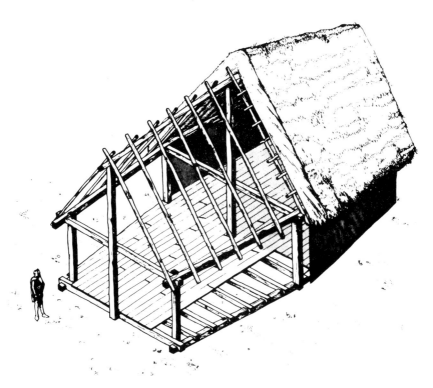

3. A possible reconstruction of a Saxon house at St. Neots (*taken from P.V. Addyman, CAS 1972, ©CAS*).

Evidence of Saxon occupation outside the settlement includes the literary references to the foundation of a religious house in the late tenth century which decayed in the eleventh century and was refounded after the Conquest. The earliest recognised archaeological features of the priory were of the thirteenth century, but seventh-century pottery and a coin were found on the site. Our final evidence for Saxon occupation is the only burial site found so far in this area. This dates to the early Saxon period and consisted of mixed inhumations and cremations found with two urns and two brooches and is well away from any known habitation.

Religious Sites

Pagan Saxon Burials

Probably the richest class of archaeological objects of all periods found in Cambridgeshire are the grave goods which were deposited with pagan burials. These stand in stark contrast to the evidence of the contemporary habitation sites which appear so poor and infrequent but they are perhaps not so surprising when we remember that the same people built the dykes and that in the next few centuries the religious zeal which made them set such store by gifts for the dead led to the foundation of churches and religious houses. There are many problems concerned with the interpretation of these burials, some due to the nature of the evidence itself which represents only one small facet of human activity, and others due to the way so may of the cemeteries have come to light. Most of the larger sites were found in the last century, frequently by labourers working on the coprolite mines, and even the finds which were saved (generally only the jewellery which was so obviously valuable) often found their way to museums via the workmen's pockets and antique shops. Nearly all the sites have been found unexpectedly and by non-archaeologists, though some have been properly excavated after their discovery.

Accepting, therefore, that our evidence is incomplete, we must see what can be learnt from these cemeteries besides appreciating that the grave goods are beautiful museum pieces well worth examination as art objects in their own right. The first thing one might expect to learn concerns the distribution of population. The cemeteries show that settlement in Cambridgeshire was concentrated on the Cam valley, but the relationship of cemetery to settlement is complicated. Some groups obviously placed more emphasis on burial rituals than others, even apart from differences in disposable wealth. It is also now clear that many villages might use the same cemetery which could be at some distance from their habitation site and therefore one can neither plot settlement distribution nor estimate probable village size from the evidence of the burials. Therefore, whether the sites contain 'many hundreds' of skeletons, such as those at Barrington, St John's College cricket field and Girton, or have only one or two individuals they can give only the vague information that there were pagan Saxons living in the area. Evidence for the dating of the earliest settlements is more satisfactory, since the grave goods are fairly easily dated and as some are found belonging to the late fourth century they are extremely useful when looking for the earliest settlers.

The cemeteries give certain details about burial rituals and a belief in an after-life, but it is impossible to make generalised statements about these rituals because there was evidently so much variation. Cremation and inhumation are both common and are often found in the same cemetery in graves of contemporary date, and accompanied by similar classes of grave goods. Cremations were often placed in decorated burial urns and inhumations seem generally to have been laid out flat and aligned north-south but other positions and directions have been noted. Occasionally there are traces of the coffin and graves are rarely cut through early burials which must mean they were marked in some way. The grave goods clearly showed that there was a great respect for the dead, which probably implies tight family bonds

4. Grave-goods: (a) necklace (length 52 cms) and (b) brooch (length 13 cms) from cemetery at Little Wilbraham, (c) accessory urn (height 7.5 cms) from Barrington. Now in Cambridge Museum of Archaeology and Ethnology (*photo D. Hall*).

as well as a possible fear of their angry ghosts, but they can hardly be seen as sensible provisions for a life after death. Men were usually accompanied by their weapons but women often had only their jewellery although occasionally workboxes and small tools such as spindle whorls, tweezers and shears are found. Animal bones have been occasionally recognised and some of the vessels probably contained drink, but the normal grave goods, even with rich burials, seem to represent little more than their very best clothes and accoutrements and were intended to define the status not the religious beliefs of the corpse. This status equates to the person's position in life and so one can make a few generalised statements about the social hierarchy. There was a considerable difference between the rich and the poor, although there was not a return to the common Iron Age situation where the poor were simply not buried. Both men and women might have very rich burials which is in accord with the high status of women in Saxon society when we enter the historic period. Some children also had rich graves but this is less common.

If we had the skeletons from all the graves discovered we should have a good picture of the physique and mortality rates of the early Saxons and some ideas of the diseases from which they suffered. These skeletons rarely survive, however, and were not usually examined and commented upon when excavated. When they are described they are generally said to be those of people of large physique and mostly under thirty years of age.

The grave goods themselves can tell a great deal about Anglo-Saxon life quite apart from their context in burials, and demonstrate the wealth and craftsmanship common amongst these peasant settlers. They illustrate international trading patterns, for there was amber from the Baltic, cowrie shells from the Indian Ocean and amethysts, crystal, garnets and ivory from other exotic sources. The brooches and buckles which were found in position on the skeletons help us to reconstruct the rest of their dress and we also have their weapons. Unfortunately other tools very rarely occur.

The details of all the cemeteries with their burials and grave goods have already been catalogued and discussed in detail so it is not necessary to describe them here. It is probably of interest, however, to present simple lists of the items which have been found.

The jewellery found includes: bronze buckles and brooches mostly cruciform or circular in shape (these are the most common finds), one gilt mount set with garnets, silver and electron pendants, silver finger rings (sometimes spiral), beads of amber and of blue, yellow and black glass, 'girdle hangers' (which were probably originally small tools for housewives and became ornamental), crystal balls in bronze mountings, amethysts, an ivory ring, a Kimmeridge shale bangle, and a beaver tooth set in bronze.

Weapons were more conservative. Iron spears and shield bosses were by far the most common, but there are also two-edged swords and occasional axes.

The only tools found have been small shears and tweezers, toilet implements, keys, spindle whorls, decorated bone combs, a small hammer with a whetstone, and, very commonly, iron knives.

Other items include decorated pottery burial urns, occasional Roman pottery and coins, animal bones including the skeleton of a horse, bronze bindings from wooden buckets, a disc from a hanging bowl, one complete bronze hanging-bowl, iron mountings from a wooden bed, glass beakers, ivory purse rings and a bronze bell. The most recent cemetery find occurred in June 1977 when a workman on the A604 near Dry Drayton unearthed the superb decorated glass beaker illustrated on p.22. The site was visited by the writer and many human bones were found but as these belonged to a medieval gallows site and no further artifacts were discovered it was impossible to be

◁ 5. Pagan Saxon beaker of greenish glass, with trail decoration in clear and reddish-brown glass, found near Dry Drayton during improvements to the A604 (height 19.5 cms) (photo K. Drummond).

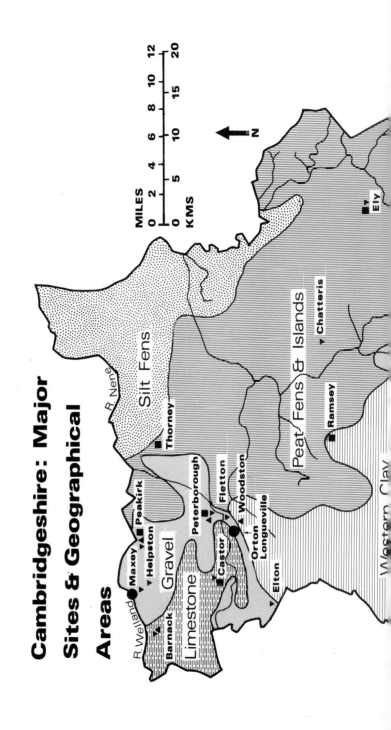

Cambridgeshire: Major Sites & Geographical Areas

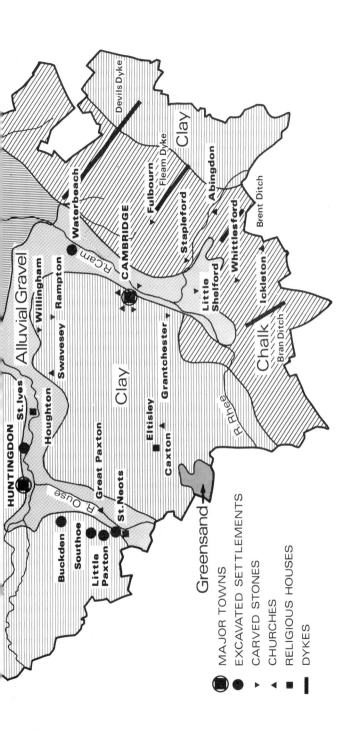

MAJOR TOWNS
EXCAVATED SETTLEMENTS
CARVED STONES
CHURCHES
RELIGIOUS HOUSES
DYKES

HUNTINGDON
St.Ives
Buckden
Southoe
Little Paxton
St.Neots
Great Paxton
Houghton
Willingham
Swavesey
Rampton
Eltisley
Caxton
Grantchester
Waterbeach
CAMBRIDGE
Fulbourn
Stapleford
Abingdon
Little Shelford
Whittlesford
Ickleton

Devils Dyke
Fleam Dyke
Brent Ditch
Bran Ditch

Clay
Alluvial Gravel
Clay
Chalk
Greensand

R.Cam
R.Ouse
R.Rhee

6. Great Paxton church. The fabric is now mostly 15th c. but contains features of the Saxon minster that was probably built by Edward the Confessor who held the manor here. The clerestory windows are Saxon and it can be seen how the later tower has cut away half of the westernmost window. The original church extended further towards the west and about 10ft further north. Inside, two bays of the nave-walls, one arch, some steps and the jambs of two more arches of the original church can be seen (*photo D. Hall*).

certain of the nature of the original site, although earlier reports of iron weapons from this site make it likely there was a small cemetery here originally.

Churches

Cambridgeshire has no outstanding Saxon churches and none which is still substantially Saxon in fabric, but thirteen retain recognisable architectural work of this period, some of which is decorative carving of exceptional interest. At Barnack church for example, the west angles of the nave are Saxon and so are the lower two stages of the tower. In Peterborough Cathedral the base of the Saxon church's walls of Barnack stone remain beneath the floor of the south transept. These can now be visited through an especially constructed subway. The Saxon walls, still several courses high, are apparently of two periods. The early walls are enormous well-laid blocks

7. St Bene't's Church, Cambridge. Saxon tower arch.

surmounted by smaller, more irregular stones, thought to represent St Ethelwold's rebuilding.

Great Paxton has more than two bays of the main walls of the nave dating to the mid eleventh century complete with arcades and clerestory windows as well as details such as jambs and an arch. Swavesey contains internal evidence of a small aisleless Saxon church and Peakirk still has the long narrow proportions and thin walls of a Saxon nave. Woodston has a small piece of Saxon walling with a double-splayed round headed window enclosed in the Victorian west tower. Cambridge is best known for St Bene't's with its famous west tower and unusual ornament on the tower arch and its Saxon chancel which was almost complete until 1872, but Saxon work has also been recognised at the Victorian brick church of St Giles which is on the site of an earlier one that had stood until 1875. The chancel arch is preserved as an arch separating the south aisle from the east chapel. Saxon fabric has also been recorded in churches at Abington, Ickleton and Caxton.

Religious Houses

The monastery at Peterborough, known originally as Medhamstede, was founded, as the name implies, on a favourable patch of meadowland, by a high-born monk (Sexwulf) in the mid seventh century, according to the *Anglo-Saxon Chronicle*. He had the support of Penda, the pagan king of Mercia, and his Christian successors and the monastery was able to grow over the next two centuries and set up cells at Brixworth and Thorney, playing a large part in the conversion of the southern midlands. Then in 870 the Danes attacked. The monks were slain and the buildings, including the church and library, were looted and then burnt. The site lay ruined until the religious revival under Edgar when it was restored in 972 by Ethelwold, Bishop of Winchester, with Adulph, the king's chancellor, as abbot. He and his successors were evidently energetic men and the monastery soon regained its power and reputation. Early in the eleventh century the name was changed to Peterborough, after the patron saint and the fortifying wall built round the precinct. There were further Danish attacks under Sweyn in 1013 but then peace until the attacks by Hereward in the Conquest period.

A neighbouring nunnery at Castor is also said to have been built in the seventh century. The facts concerning this foundation are uncertain as it is not specifically described in Bede's *History* but it seems that Penda had a Christian daughter Kyneburgha who became an abbess, and by the fourteenth century at least her nunnery was said to be located at Castor. It is not known how long this foundation lasted but it is unlikely to have survived the Danish attacks of 870. Recent excavations[10] near the church have produced possible hut sites and occupation material that would fit the period of around 655 to 870. The signs seem to suggest female occupation with quite a high standard of living. They include iron knives, shears, a fine bronze wrist clip, a stone spindle whorl, a bone pin beater for weaving, a decorated bone comb and fragments of other bone pins and glass possibly from vessels. Other Saxon remains are the Saxon portion and monumental stone in the church.

Another religious lady in this area was St Pega, the sister of St Guthlac who founded Crowland. She is supposed to have retired to a hermitage at

Peakirk after burying her brother and before dying in Rome in 716. The village was named after her and the church of St Pega's contains a Saxon cross-base and fragments of a monument rather like the Hedda stone. Other nunneries in Cambridgeshire founded in Saxon times were Chatteris and probably Eltisley, but very little is known about either of these. Chatteris was founded early in the eleventh century by Aelfwen, Queen of East Anglia, who was the first abbess, and her brother Ednoth, second abbot of Ramsey, but the lands given were few and the nunnery continued to be fairly small and poor throughout the Middle Ages. At Eltisley we have only the tradition that there was a Saxon nunnery where St Pandiona, a Scottish princess, died and which was later moved to Hinchingbrook.

Ramsey Abbey was a later foundation than Peterborough but was still able to grow into one of the largest landowners of the Middle Ages. Traditionally it was founded about 969 by Aylwin, foster-brother of King Edgar, with the help of St Oswald of Worcester. It was well endowed by royal personages and became an important centre of learning and education. The Abbey was rebuilt in the Middle Ages before it was almost entirely destroyed by the Cromwell family at the Dissolution, so the only remains now visible are the medieval gatehouse and the lower part of what is now a boundary wall and various fragments now incorporated in the present building.

Thorney was another abbey that grew rich and respected due to royal patronage. Sexwulf, first abbot of Peterborough, is said to have established a community of hermits there because it was such a remote and wild place. Little more is heard of this early community, except for the names of some saints who lived there, such as Tatwin who rowed Guthlac to Thorney for which he is commemorated as one of the figures on the west front of Crowland Abbey. Thorney was destroyed by the Danes, and then in 972 St Ethelwold, Bishop of Winchester, decided that it was suitably secluded for meditation and prayer during Lent and established a monastery there, with King Edgar as patron and protector. He began to collect saintly relics, sometimes by rather dubious means such as carrying off the bones of St Etheldreda's chaplain from Chatteris Nunnery. Among the benefactors of this abbey who are known to have stayed there are Cnut, his wife Emma and his sons Harold and Harthacnut. The abbey was despoiled by Earl Godwyn during a rebellion under Edward the Confessor and then again by Hereward but it was obviously still very wealthy in 1085 when there was a great rebuilding involving the destruction of the Saxon church. The Dissolution meant the destruction of the monastic buildings apart from the church and nothing of the Saxon architecture has been discovered. Many of the stones went to build Trinity and Corpus Christi Colleges.

Ely was yet another very early foundation supported by royalty which was to become an extremely wealthy landowner in the Middle Ages and to survive, like Peterborough, as a cathedral. Etheldreda, a princess of East Anglia, fled to this remote spot and founded a monastery in 673 when her second husband Egfrith, king of Northumberland, began to insist that she lose her virginity after thirteen years of marriage. The monastery was for both sexes, not an uncommon arrangement at this time, and seems to have been ruled by women, including Etheldreda's sister, St Sexburg, widow of the King of Mercia. The community was destroyed by the Danes, but a college of secular priests remained on the spot and so impressed Edgar that he encouraged Ethelwold of Winchester to re-establish the monastery, endowing it with very wide estates and other rich gifts. Brithnoth, leader of the Saxon forces against the Danes, was so well entertained in Ely after having been disappointed with his reception at Ramsey that he added greatly to these gifts, and a collection of relics was acquired often by rather unholy means such as agreeing to protect the bones of St Alban during Danish raids and then returning the wrong ones when the danger was past. Cnut and Emma were especially fond of Ely and there are stories of Cnut listening with pleasure to the monks singing as he rowed past, and it was here that Edward the Confessor was educated.

Priories were founded before the Conquest at St Neots and St Ives and both were to become successful market towns, partly by the coincidence that they were well placed for communications and partly because the holy relics attracted many visitors. Neither became important as a seat of learning and so they did not produce their own chronicles like the larger houses; very little is therefore known of their early histories and these became very confused with legend. St Neots was probably not founded before 972 when Earl Leofric and his wife with the assistance of St Oswald of Worcester brought monks from Thorney and Ely and established a house that was subject to Ely. They acquired the bones of St Neot from Cornwall, by tradition because the saint complained in a vision that he was being neglected and so his relics were handed over by their warden to Leofric. The house may well have suffered in the Danish invasions of 1010, but there were a few monks there after the Conquest who were displaced by Normans. St Ives has even less of any real history. The priory was in existence by the Conquest but all that is known of its early history is the legend that the bones of St Ivo, a Persian bishop who travelled widely, were found in a field near Slepe around 1000 AD by one of the Abbot of Ramsey's ploughmen. The saint appeared in a vision to strike a disbelieving bailiff with rheumatic gout which led the monks of Ramsey to build a suitable shrine near the site. The priory continued to be ruled by Ramsey and always seems to have remained very small with just a single priest by the time of the Dissolution.

8. Devil's Dyke. View along Devil's Dyke towards Newmarket Heath, at the section ▷
   where the Newmarket bypass has now been cut (*photo R. Tibbs*).

Warfare

The Dykes

The importance of warfare and the frequent need for massive defensive measures at many points in Saxon history is clear from the poetry and histories of the time. There were the initial invasions which are still so imperfectly understood, the wars between rival kingdoms until Alfred achieved unity, and the raids, settlements and final conquest by the Danes. This meant that although many peasants might live without direct contact with raids or battles, society had to be organised so that maximum military power was available for political survival. Out of all the bloodshed, heroism, legal and social obligations, royal marriages and stratagems this involved, the clear physical evidence of the dykes remains.

These dykes[11-19] are easy to describe: they have been frequently excavated and much discussed; their basic function is obvious, but their accurate date, political context, the part they played and in what campaign, are still beyond our modern archaeological and historical techniques to decide. They are four in number (the Mile Ditch, although superficially similar, has a different strategic function and is probably of the Iron Age), each consisting of a large bank and ditch with probably a small outer bank, and they were built to defend people on the East Anglian side by cutting off the Icknield Way,

9. Devil's Dyke, during the excavation by B. Hope-Taylor, 1973 (*photo R.Tibbs*).

joining up the all but impassable forests and fenlands on either side of the chalk ridge.

Devil's Dyke is the most impressive archaeological monument in Cambridgeshire and is the largest, though not the longest, of this type of site in Britain. It is 7½ miles long, running from the fen edge at Reach to Woodditton where the previously forested clay plateau of south-east Cambridgeshire and Essex begins. Originally it slightly overlapped Reach Lode (a Roman canal), although the far end was levelled in the Middle Ages to make way for the Hythe and Fair Green, giving a continuous defence ten miles long and joining up with the Cam. Its length is basically straight, apart from two intentional changes in direction, although it includes several very minor bends and it is tactically sited to give the best defensive line. Accurate surveying techniques and a good knowledge of the terrain were obviously available.

The dyke today still stands about 12 — 15 ft high along most of its length, and up to 70ft wide, with a ditch 17ft deep and 65ft wide on its south west side. A number of gaps have been cut through, but probably none were original causeways. The profile of the dyke must always have been fairly irregular, probably due to the employment of different gangs of workers, while in many places later quarrying and ploughing have affected its surviving appearance.

Almost nothing was known about the dyke, which, it was thought, was most likely Iron Age in date, until 1923 when Cyril Fox cut a section through it near the Roman villa site at Reach. Sealed underneath the bank he found many sherds of third century pottery and a Roman coin. The pottery consisted of very small abraded fragments which had obviously been rolled around in plough soil for many years before being covered over, and this gave conclusive proof that the dyke was either very late or post-Roman. The excavation also showed that there had been a low marker bank of topsoil, but the dyke itself was constructed in one short space of time and was never enlarged.

In the next fifty years there was much speculation and excavations were carried out on the other dykes, but further work on Devil's Dyke had to wait until 1973 when Brian Hope-Taylor investigated another section in advance of construction of the Newmarket bypass. The nature of this sort of earthwork means that even large scale excavation cannot really hope to find close dating evidence or details of function without a great stroke of luck such as the discovery of some datable object that was thrown away or lost while the bank was being thrown up. No such discovery was made, the only finds being a coin of about 350 AD beneath the bank and a medieval burial cut into the ditch fill, which do not help very much to reduce the date limits for construction.

Valuable engineering details, however, were noted. The marker bank, for

10. Devil's Dyke after excavation. Note the differing geology of the tip-lines and the dark "marker bank" of old top-soil. The bank was symmetrical but at this point a large slice has been taken out of one side at a later date (*photo R. Tibbs*).

example, was only made of top soil from the immediate area, so the top soil from the ditch must have gone to make an outer bank, whose existence was further suggested by the way the ditch had silted up. It was also obvious from the way that the distinctive geological layers in the natural chalk were reproduced several times over in the bank that this had been built up strip by strip longitudinally, while the visible tip lines showed that the quarry material must have been hoisted in great tips to the top of the bank on earth-hauling ramps by some mechanism.

The Fleam Dyke is a smaller defence and has certain structural differences, but its southern sector is clearly part of the same system and must be roughly contemporary. It is only 3 miles 520 yards long and cuts off the chalk highway between Balsham and Fulbourn Fen, thus serving much the same function as the Devil's Dyke but needing only half the number of defenders. Its present dimensions are 85ft in overall width, with a ditch 11ft deep and bank 11ft high where it is reasonably well preserved, so it must have been a formidable barrier, especially as it could be better manned than Devil's Dyke. This could mean that it was either earlier or later depending on which side was more successful during the campaigns for which they were constructed.

The dyke was first examined by Cyril Fox and W.M. Palmer who cut seven sections through it near Mutlow Hill and Newmarket Road in 1921. No dating evidence turned up, all the finds being Roman from a known Roman building near by. The excavators found an original bank about 7ft high that was increased by two additions after a considerable interval and also evidence of various minor repairs and improvements. In the area examined the ditch was 15ft deep and the bank still stood to 11ft.

In 1971 a water pipeline was cut through the dyke and the University Field Club took the opportunity to examine another section. They found a small deposit of rubble that might have been a marking out bank similar to that found beneath Devil's Dyke, and they noticed that the fill of the ditch suggested that there had originally been an outer bank, again reminiscent of Devil's Dyke. There was a very thick layer of silt where the ditch had been allowed to fill up naturally and then clean chalk, perhaps thrown in when the outer bank was levelled.

The Bran or Heydon Ditch extends from clayland at Heydon to the site of the mere at Fowlmere, and although it was obviously much slighter than Fleam and Devil's Dyke, its dating evidence has proved to be very similar, for when Cyril Fox excavated there he found Roman pottery dating to the third century. This dyke has been levelled along most of its length and is now followed by hedgerows, parish boundaries and slight undulations, but Fox showed that there had been a ditch that was up to 8ft deep and 22ft wide. T.C. Lethbridge and W.M. Palmer returned to Fox's excavation after he had found two skeletons and were able to find over fifty more as well as two earlier shallow ditches with a palisade between them which seemed to form the earliest defence along this line.

The skeletons they found were mature males apart from two probable females and a new-born child. Most of them showed signs of a violent death by beheading, pole-axing, being hanged or having their throats cut. Skulls were often found separated from bodies and many were very decayed before burial. The site was in use over a long period. There were scarcely any artifacts apart from an iron knife and clip and a few late Saxon sherds. which probably means that they were buried unclothed. The lack of grave goods and the east-west alignment of most of the skeletons suggest a Christian date. The excavators thought these skeletons were the result of a massacre of the Bran Ditch defenders but David Hill reconsidered them in a recent *PCAS* article and decided they must be the result of a 'cwealmstow', or Saxon execution site, where suicides and unbaptised children would also be buried. The Saxon punishment for many crimes according to the surviving laws was to be left hanging until the flesh rotted from the bones, a punishment which would seem to fit the facts about these burials very well.

Brent or Pampisford Ditch has not yet been dated but seems to belong to the same series. It is 1½ miles long running from an upland spar in Abington

Park to a springhead in Pampisford. Parts of the ditch are still as deep as 7ft but there is no bank remaining.

Weapons

The normal weapons were spears and shields, and it is spear heads which are found in the greatest numbers in pagan graves and as stray finds from the Fens. The heads of the spears, which were also used for hunting, were fairly uniform in shape but vary in length from a few inches to two feet. The wooden shafts are scarcely ever found but contemporary illustrations show that they were normally longer than the height of a man. The shields seem to have been light round wooden boards, sometimes covered with leather with a hollow in the centre for the hand, which in the better examples would be covered by an iron boss. These bosses are quite commonly found in graves.

Another common weapon that probably served more often as a tool was the 'scramasax', a single-edged dagger carried in a sheath at a man's thigh. Its length might vary from that of a small knife to almost that of a sword. Like other weapons it was occasionally elaborately decorated but it was generally of plain iron.

Axes were also mainly used for peaceful ends, but they might also be used in hand-to-hand fighting, as shown in the Bayeux tapestry. 'Franciscas', or throwing axes, which were quite common on the Continent, also occasionally occur.

The weapon of greatest prestige was the sword. These are frequently eulogized in poems such as *Beowulf* and evidently became important heirlooms, reserved for warriors of the higher classes. They were two-edged, nearly three feet long and were carried at the waist in a scabbard made of two thin lengths of wood covered with leather, sometimes with ornamental metal at the mouth. Most were beaten from one piece of iron, but the best were 'pattern welded' with bands of iron twisted together and beaten flat to give a very sharp, flexible and strong weapon. A few of the blades were

11. (a) Viking sword from Stanground (length 93 cms) (b) Spear-head provenance unknown (length 38 cms) (c) Spear-head from the fens (length 35 cms). Now in Wisbech Museum (*photo D. Hall*).

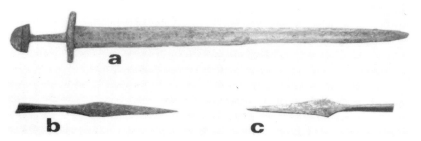

decorated, and occasionally carried the names of the maker and owner, and some had elaborate pommels, but most were simple iron weapons with grips of bone or wood.

Other items that appear on illustrations or are mentioned in poetry are bows and arrows, helmets and chain mail. These are scarcely ever found archaeologically and do not occur in Cambridgeshire, the nearest example of helmet and chain mail being found at Sutton Hoo. Evidently they were very rare and the normal soldier would probably be protected by a leather tunic and cap.

Art and Industry

Anglo-Saxon art is a vast theme and it is only possible within this chapter to touch upon its significance in terms of its functions, its indications of the social organisation and contacts, and the objects which can still be seen today. Art and industry are described together because art was the responsibility of professional craftsmen working in national and international styles probably in quite considerable workshops, while organised industry generally provided articles that could not be made locally which usually meant luxury items of high artistic standard.

Many Saxon designs are based on animal forms in the abstract, with their shapes broken up into tortuous patterns. They are mostly influenced by abstract Germanic styles in the early period but Celtic patterns, partly indigenous and partly re-imported from Ireland, and classical naturalism from the Mediterranean soon became important, with a result that was totally Saxon. In later years the Viking influence became strong.

The art which survives from the pagan period is connected with jewellery and personal articles generally found in graves. Brooches are the most common items and show the greatest artistic variety and skill with metalwork.

In the Christian period most of the art is religious. Metalwork continued and although the best surviving metal objects were sacred, such as chalices and crosses, jewellery probably continued to be just as popular although changes in burial practice meant that it has rarely survived. Occasional discoveries such as the Alfred Jewel show that the standard of work was extremely high and from Cambridgeshire we have a tenth century silver brooch from Sutton, now in the British Museum, which is decorated with animal and snake patterns with a curse written on the back. We also have a remarkable jewelled pendant made of crystal, gold, garnet and amethyst coloured glass, dating to around 600-700, probably ploughed out near the Saxon cemetery at Ely. It is Christian in character and most likely belonged to a wealthy Christian princess, St Etheldreda being one obvious possibility.

Major new art forms introduced from the Mediterranean with Christianity were writing, with all the attendant illuminated illustrations, and stone

12. Carvings on Old Fletton church (a) looking north (b) looking west.

13. Carving on east wall of Old Fletton church (*photo D. Hall*).

14. Illuminated letter from the 10th c. Ramsey Psalter (*Now in the British Museum and reproduced by permission of the British Library Board*).

carving, both ornamental and architectural. Writing was the responsibility of the religious houses and thanks to them we have many histories, poems, homilies, charters and laws surviving and the glorious illuminated manuscripts.

Stone carving was used for churches, crosses and grave slabs and for decorative purposes often connected with religion. It is usually found incorporated in churches. The production of monumental decoratively carved stones was an important industry in East Anglia that seems to have been centred on Cambridge.[20]

The stones included free-standing crosses possibly used as centres of worship before churches were built, and slabs to cover the graves of the wealthy. They were nearly all carved from Barnack stone and were decorated with designs involving plait work or interlacing patterns, arranged in panels. Most of the stones probably date to the late tenth to the early eleventh century and are now most commonly found incorporated in the fabric of churches.

The crosses, which were lavishly decorated and seem to have been between 2ft 8ins and 4ft high with circular heads, are found all over East Anglia and probably came from one workshop. One was found beneath the rampart of Cambridge Castle and another beneath the floor of Fulbourn church (both now in the Archaeology and Ethnology Museum), a base and shaft are still in Stapleford church and fragmentary examples are built into the church-porch at Willingham and Barnack church tower. Fragments occur in Peterborough Cathedral, two stand in Elton churchyard, there is a base in Castor church, a shaft in the chapel of Peakirk and fragments at Helpston.

Fragments of decorated grave slabs, generally built into church walls, have been recognised at Little St Mary's in Cambridge, at Grantchester, Little Shelford, Stretham, Whittlesford, Willingham, Rampton, Helpston, Maxey and Barnack. Restoration work in Peterborough Cathedral in 1888 led to the discovery of several grave slabs which are particularly important because two were still in their original position and so we are able to learn that the graves were for laymen, for they were on the north side of the church while monks were on the south, and it could be seen how the graves were arranged with the bodies laid straight in the earth, the decorated slabs flat above them and headstones carved with a cross and footstones in position. Similar headstones and footstones have been found in Cambridge, Helpston and Barnack and were presumably arranged in the same way.

One unique memorial is St Ovin's cross, which was returned to Ely in the eighteenth century after it was discovered being used as a mounting block in Haddenham. The Latin inscription is still decipherable and reads "O God, grant thy light and rest to Ovin. Amen", in commemoration of Etheldreda's steward Ovin, who died in 676. It stands in Ely Cathedral.

The art of decorative sculpture was also well developed in Cambridgeshire in the Saxon period, especially in the eighth century, and many fragments have also survived because they have been built into churches. Most of them are evidently part of larger friezes which were probably ecclesiastical in function although the subject matter was not necessarily religious. It seems likely that the workshops producing this high quality work, which is also found in Northamptonshire, were centred on Peterborough.

Peterborough Cathedral itself contains some outstanding stone sculpture, some of which dates to the eighth century. Architectural fragments were found beneath the Norman floor during reconstruction work in the nineteenth century, as well as many grave-slabs and cross-shafts. Decorative carvings include the famous Hedda stone, named after the abbot who was killed in 870 but dating probably to the eighth century, which is carved with six saintly figures standing in arches beneath a decorated gabled sloping roof, and also a slab with two figures that are similar to those of the Hedda stone but of a more martial character. The function of the stones is not known but it is likely they were shrines placed above holy relics beside the altar.

Equally important carved stones are now to be found in the industrial suburb of Fletton, although it is likely they were taken from Peterborough Cathedral after one of its early fires. The stones, which are now built into

15. Left: Virgin weeping – from the Crucifixion scene in the Ramsey Psalter
(*reproduced by permission of the British Library Board*, Harley Ms. 2904, f. 3v)
Right – a 9th c. carving in Castor church (height 50 cms) (*photo D. Hall*).

16. Gilt bronze disc brooch from Upton, near Peterborough, now in Peterborough Museum, diameter 6.3 cms (*copyright, Peterborough Museum*).

a buttress, are carved with imaginary birds and beasts and three heads under arches in a very minute and detailed style which Pevsner describes as "lively, even humorous".

Fragments of other friezes survive at Castor, where there is a small carving of a man standing beneath an arch, and in the chapel of St John in Ely where a rather indistinct representation of a man sitting on an ox blowing a trumpet has been inserted above a doorway.

A different kind of carved decoration is also found directly related to the architecture of churches. Barnack Tower is the best example, ornamented with a sun dial, projecting beasts' heads and three stone slabs with rich carvings in high relief of birds, vines and acanthus leaves. There is a lion mask of ca. 900 on Glatton church, and in St Bene't's, Cambridge, lions have been carved above the pillars of the internal Saxon arch. The exception to all this Christian work is the obscene carving (here of a woman and a horse) of the type known as a "sheila-na-gig" that is now built into the spire of Whittlesford church.

Extremely delicate carvings in other materials, particularly walrus ivory, were also produced, again often with religious connections. Saintly bones, for example, which were so highly prized, were housed in precious and elaborately decorated caskets. One superb example is the Gandersheim casket of carved ivory which is now in the Herzog Anton-Ulrich Museum in Brunswick but which was apparently made for use in Ely for an inscription in runes on the bottom reads "Holy Virgin be thou a light to Ely". The casket has interlace patterns and interwined animals and probably dates to the late eighth century.

According to written sources, which are borne out by the few surviving fragments, Saxon England also had a high reputation for other arts such as woodwork, painting, stained glass and embroidery.

17. (a) Large square-headed brooch from Haslingfield (length 17 cms) (b) One of a pair of cruciform brooches from Newnham (length 13.5 cms) Cambridge Museum of Archaeology and Ethnology (*photo D. Hall*).

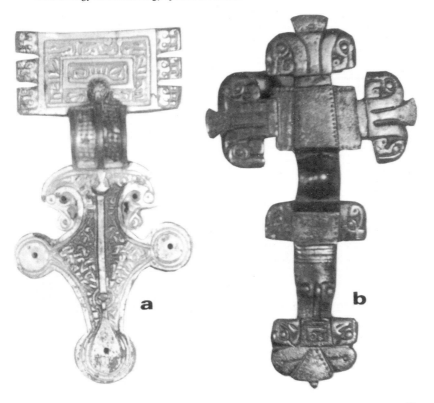

18. Lower two stages of Barnack church. Note the typical long and short stonework at the corners, the vertical pilaster strips, the round window heads carved from single stones, the round-headed door and the intricately-carved decorations, although some of these are too small to show in the photograph (*photo D. Hall*).

19. The Gandersheim casket. An 8th c. casket of carved bone and bronze with a runic inscription on the base meaning "Holy Virgin be thou a light to Ely". Now in the Herzog Anton-Ulrich Museum, Brunswick.

At a different level from these high-class cultural and religious functions, industries existed to supply farming and household needs. The importance of the smiths has become legendary and carpenters and potters must also have been important figures in the local community, for iron, wood and pottery provided most of the materials needed by the peasant communities. Wood, of course, scarcely ever survives but the high standard of workmanship is testified by illustrations of fortifications, buildings and ships, the success of the Viking ships and the navy which Alfred built to fight them, and the house plans detected by excavation which are the remains of mighty aisled halls. Iron objects would normally be re-smelted and generally survive only as grave goods and occasional stray finds, therefore weapons are common and tools extremely rare. A hoard from Westley Waterless contained in a decorative lead vat now in the Archaeology and Ethnology Museum contained a plough-share and some tools which were probably used by a carpenter.

Pottery[21, 22, 23] is easily broken but the fragments are indestructible and very common so their study is important to the archaeologist. Early Saxon pottery is almost identical to that found in the Anglo-Saxon homelands and marks a complete change from the Roman standardized wheelmade wares produced in industrial areas such as Horningsea and the Nene Valley, which depended on safe and extensive trade routes and organised labour. The new pottery was all handmade apart from occasional 'Romano-Saxon' wares which survived for a short period in parts of Britain although they have so far not been identified in Cambridgeshire, and was mostly in very simple baggy shapes with straight rims. The common ware in Cambridgeshire is sometimes tempered with finely ground pebbles and is so featureless that the plain sherds are easily confused with prehistoric pottery. Finer wares are very distinctive with elaborate shapes, raised decorations in corrugated lines on the necks and shoulders, applied bosses and rosette stamps and sometimes a burnished surface. The stamps are particularly interesting because identical ones are found on groups of pots within the region and this points to the existence of professional potters and to the development of internal trade. The decorated pottery was most commonly used for burial urns although fragments have also been found on domestic sites.

In the middle Saxon period a slow potter's wheel came into use in a few centres such as Ipswich, where large-scale production took place using kilns, some of which have been excavated. Ipswich ware, which has a hard, sandy fabric and usually occurs as small cooking pots and spouted pitchers, was distributed along the coast and only occasionally found its way into Cambridge. Elsewhere in Cambridgeshire the plain handmade wares continued until the late Saxon period when kilns making Thetford ware, Stamford ware and St Neots ware came into production. Kilns have rarely been located but were probably quite widespread, not necessarily centred on the towns whose names archaeologists have adopted for the types of pottery. A fast wheel was used and the pottery, known collectively as Saxo-Norman ware because it is indistinguishable from that in use after the Conquest, is based on styles introduced from the Rhineland and became the most common ware in East Anglia and the east Midlands. The forms are varied and sometimes quite elaborate, including spouted pitchers, storage jars, cooking pots, costrels and lamps and bowls with inturned rims. Thetford ware has a sandy fabric and is common in Norfolk, Suffolk and Essex. It occurs in Cambridge and, sparsely, over the rest of the county. Stamford ware has a smooth pale fabric and was commonly decorated with a light yellow or pale green or occasionally orange glaze. This glaze seems to be the first known in Europe since Roman times and was probably introduced directly from Byzantium. This pottery, which is found throughout the east Midlands, occurs all over Cambridgeshire, especially in the towns along the river valleys. St Neots ware is the most common late Saxon pottery in Cambridgeshire. It is a fairly soft, shell-tempered ware varying from buff to black in colour, often with a distinctive purplish tinge.

Conclusion

In 1066 William narrowly defeated the Saxon army and afterwards England can be described as "medieval". The royal dynasty and most of the upper classes changed, the immediate influences on cultural and political developments became French and Continental rather than Scandinavian, and there was a Norman impact on social and agricultural organisation which is still debated. The land he conquered, however, had stable settlements and had reached a high level of civilization and economic development, and thus a great many of the significant features of Saxon England were to endure into modern times.

References

1. C.F. Tebbutt & T.C. Lethbridge, 'Huts of the Anglo-Saxon period', in *CAS* XXXIII, 1933, p.137.
2. C.M. Coote, 'A Saxon Hut at Houghton', in *Transactions of the Cambs. and Hunts. Archaeological Society*, 7, 1950, p.71.
3. P.V. Addyman, 'A Dark Age settlement at Maxey, Northants.' *in Medieval Archaeology* VIII, 1964, p.20.
4. P.V. Addyman, 'Late Saxon settlements in the St. Neots area II' in *CAS* LXII, 1969, p.59.
5. T.C. Lethbridge & C.F. Tebbutt, 'Preliminary investigations of an early medieval moated site at Manor Farm, Southoe, Hunts.' in *CAS* XXXVIII, 1936, p.158.
6. C.F. Tebbutt, 'An eleventh-century 'boat-shaped' building at Buckden' in *CAS* LV, 1961, p.13.
7. P.V. Addyman & M. Biddle, 'Medieval Cambridge: recent finds and excavations' in *CAS* LVIII, 1965, p.74.
8. H. Cam, 'The origin of the borough of Cambridge: a consideration of Prof. Carl Stephenson's theories' in *CAS* XXXV, 1934, p.33.
9. P.V. Addyman, 'Late Saxon settlements in the St. Neots area' in *CAS* LXIV, 1972, p.45.
10. C.G. Dallas, 'The Nunnery of St Kyneburgha at Castor', in *Durobrivae* I, 1973, p.17.
11. C. Fox, 'Excavations in the Cambridgeshire Dykes: Worstead St, Fleam Dyke', in *CAS* LXXII, 1921, p.21.
12. C. Fox & W.M. Palmer, 'Excavations in the Cambridgeshire Dykes II', in *CAS* XXIV, 1922, p.28.
13. C. Fox, 'Excavations in the Cambridgeshire Dykes III', in *CAS* XXV, 1923, p.21.
14. C. Fox, 'Excavations in the Cambridgeshire Dykes IV', in *CAS* XXVI, 1924, p.90.
15. C. Fox & W.M. Palmer, 'Excavations in the Cambridgeshire Dykes V', in *CAS* XXVII, 1925, p.16.
16. W.M. Palmer, C.S. Leaf & T.C. Lethbridge, 'Further excavations at the Bran Ditch', in *CAS* XXXII, 1930, p.54.
17. T.C. Lethbridge, 'The riddle of the dykes', in *CAS* LI, 1957, p.1.
18. M. Smith, 'A section across Fleam Dyke', in *CAS* LXIV, 1973, p.30.
19. B. Hope-Taylor & D. Hill, 'The Cambridgeshire dykes I. The Devil's Dyke investigations, II. Bran Ditch, the burials reconsidered', in *CAS* LXVI, 1976, p.123.
20. C. Fox, 'Anglo-Saxon monumental sculpture in the Cambridge Region', in *CAS* LXXI, 1920, p.15.
21. J.G. Hurst, 'Saxo-Norman pottery in East Anglia', in *CAS* XLIX, 1955, p.43.
22. J.G. Hurst, G.C. Dunning, J.N.L. Myres & F. Tischler, 'Anglo-Saxon pottery: a symposium', in *Medieval Archaeology* III, 1959, p.1.
23. J.G. Hurst, 'Saxo-Norman pottery in East Anglia', in *CAS* LI, 1957, p.7.

CAS = Proceedings of the Cambridge Antiquarian Society.

Further Reading

The major reference works are the volumes of the Royal Commission on Historical Monuments dealing with *Huntingdonshire* (1926), *Cambridge* (1955), *West Cambridgeshire* (1969), *Peterborough New Town* (1969), and *North-East Cambridgeshire* (1973); and the Victoria County History volumes devoted to *Huntingdonshire* (vols. 1–3, 1926-36) and *Cambridgeshire* (vols. 1–5, 1938-73).

Durobrivae, an annual review of Nene Valley archaeology, is available from Mrs C. Mackreth, 32 Hall Lane, Werrington, Cambs. Specialized works devoted to the Anglo-Saxon period include:

Anglo-Saxon Chronicle, trans. by G.N. Garmonsway (London, 1967)

Bede *History of the English Church and People*, trans. by L. Sherley-Price (Harmondsworth, 1955)

Fox, C. *Archaeology of the Cambridge Region* (Cambridge, 1923)

Mawer, A. & Stenton, F.M. *The Place-names of Bedfordshire and Huntingdonshire* (Cambridge, 1926)

Meaney, A. *Early Anglo-Saxon burial sites* (London, 1964)

Reaney, P.H. *The Place-names of Cambridgeshire and the Isle of Ely* (Cambridge, 1943)

Taylor, H.M. & J. *Anglo-Saxon Architecture* (Cambridge, 1965)

Wilson, D. *The Anglo-Saxons* (Harmondsworth, 1971)

Wilson, D. (*ed.*) *Anglo-Saxon England* (London, 1976)

Cambridge University Archaeology and Ethnology Museum: open 2–4 p.m., Monday – Saturday. *Curator:* P.W. Gathercole.

Peterborough Museum: open 12 a.m – 5 p.m., Tuesday – Saturday. *Archaeological Assistant*: Martin Howe.

Norris Museum, St. Ives: open March – October, 10 a.m.–5 p.m., October – March, 10 a.m.–4 p.m., Tuesday – Friday. 10–12 noon. Saturday, 2–5 p.m. Monday. (closed 1–2 p.m.). *Curator:* Christopher Morris.

Wisbech and Fenland Museum: open May – September, 10 a.m.–5p.m.; October – April, 10 a.m.–4 p.m. Tuesday – Saturday (closed 1–2 p.m.). *Curator:* Rosalinda Hardiman.

Admission free in all cases.